BUSINESS EVENT

Business/ Company

Address

Log#

Start Date

End Date

Event   Date

BUSINESS EVENT

Name of Event	
City,	
State/Zip	
Telephone	
Time Started	
Time Ended	
Date	

Item	Time	Events/Incidents	Actions Taken	Notes

Name _____ Signature _____

BUSINESS EVENT

Name of Event	
City,	
State/Zip	
Telephone	
Time Started	
Time Ended	
Date	

Item	Time	Events/Incidents	Actions Taken	Notes

Name _____ Signature_____

BUSINESS EVENT

Name of Event	
City,	
State/Zip	
Telephone	
Time Started	
Time Ended	
Date	

Item	Time	Events/Incidents	Actions Taken	Notes

Name _____ Signature _____

BUSINESS EVENT

Name of Event	
City,	
State/Zip	
Telephone	
Time Started	
Time Ended	
Date	

Item	Time	Events/Incidents	Actions Taken	Notes

Name _____ Signature _____

BUSINESS EVENT

Name of Event	
City,	
State/Zip	
Telephone	
Time Started	
Time Ended	
Date	

Item	Time	Events/Incidents	Actions Taken	Notes

Name _____Signature_____

BUSINESS EVENT

Name of Event	
City,	
State/Zip	
Telephone	
Time Started	
Time Ended	
Date	

Item	Time	Events/Incidents	Actions Taken	Notes

Name _____ Signature_____

BUSINESS EVENT

Name of Event	
City,	
State/Zip	
Telephone	
Time Started	
Time Ended	
Date	

Item	Time	Events/Incidents	Actions Taken	Notes

Name _____ Signature _____

BUSINESS EVENT

Name of Event	
City,	
State/Zip	
Telephone	
Time Started	
Time Ended	
Date	

Item	Time	Events/Incidents	Actions Taken	Notes

Name _____Signature_____

BUSINESS EVENT

Name of Event	
City,	
State/Zip	
Telephone	
Time Started	
Time Ended	
Date	

Item	Time	Events/Incidents	Actions Taken	Notes

Name _____ Signature _____

BUSINESS EVENT

Name of Event	
City,	
State/Zip	
Telephone	
Time Started	
Time Ended	
Date	

Item	Time	Events/Incidents	Actions Taken	Notes

Name _____ Signature_____

BUSINESS EVENT

Name of Event	
City,	
State/Zip	
Telephone	
Time Started	
Time Ended	
Date	

Item	Time	Events/Incidents	Actions Taken	Notes

Name _____Signature_____

BUSINESS EVENT

Name of Event	
City,	
State/Zip	
Telephone	
Time Started	
Time Ended	
Date	

Item	Time	Events/Incidents	Actions Taken	Notes

Name _____Signature_____

BUSINESS EVENT

Name of Event	
City,	
State/Zip	
Telephone	
Time Started	
Time Ended	
Date	

Item	Time	Events/Incidents	Actions Taken	Notes

Name _____Signature_____

BUSINESS EVENT

Name of Event	
City,	
State/Zip	
Telephone	
Time Started	
Time Ended	
Date	

Item	Time	Events/Incidents	Actions Taken	Notes

Name _____ Signature_____

BUSINESS EVENT

Name of Event	
City,	
State/Zip	
Telephone	
Time Started	
Time Ended	
Date	

Item	Time	Events/Incidents	Actions Taken	Notes

Name _____Signature_____

BUSINESS EVENT

Name of Event	
City,	
State/Zip	
Telephone	
Time Started	
Time Ended	
Date	

Item	Time	Events/Incidents	Actions Taken	Notes

Name _____Signature_____

BUSINESS EVENT

Name of Event	
City,	
State/Zip	
Telephone	
Time Started	
Time Ended	
Date	

Item	Time	Events/Incidents	Actions Taken	Notes

Name _____Signature_____

BUSINESS EVENT

Name of Event	
City,	
State/Zip	
Telephone	
Time Started	
Time Ended	
Date	

Item	Time	Events/Incidents	Actions Taken	Notes

Name _____Signature_____

BUSINESS EVENT

Name of Event	
City,	
State/Zip	
Telephone	
Time Started	
Time Ended	
Date	

Item	Time	Events/Incidents	Actions Taken	Notes

Name _____Signature_____

BUSINESS EVENT

Name of Event	
City,	
State/Zip	
Telephone	
Time Started	
Time Ended	
Date	

Item	Time	Events/Incidents	Actions Taken	Notes

Name _____Signature_____

BUSINESS EVENT

Name of Event	
City,	
State/Zip	
Telephone	
Time Started	
Time Ended	
Date	

Item	Time	Events/Incidents	Actions Taken	Notes

Name _____ Signature _____

BUSINESS EVENT

Name of Event	
City,	
State/Zip	
Telephone	
Time Started	
Time Ended	
Date	

Item	Time	Events/Incidents	Actions Taken	Notes

Name _____ Signature_____

BUSINESS EVENT

Name of Event	
City,	
State/Zip	
Telephone	
Time Started	
Time Ended	
Date	

Item	Time	Events/Incidents	Actions Taken	Notes

Name _____ Signature _____

BUSINESS EVENT

Name of Event	
City,	
State/Zip	
Telephone	
Time Started	
Time Ended	
Date	

Item	Time	Events/Incidents	Actions Taken	Notes

Name _____ Signature_____

BUSINESS EVENT

Name of Event	
City,	
State/Zip	
Telephone	
Time Started	
Time Ended	
Date	

Item	Time	Events/Incidents	Actions Taken	Notes

Name _____Signature_____

BUSINESS EVENT

Name of Event	
City,	
State/Zip	
Telephone	
Time Started	
Time Ended	
Date	

Item	Time	Events/Incidents	Actions Taken	Notes

Name _____ Signature_____

BUSINESS EVENT

Name of Event	
City,	
State/Zip	
Telephone	
Time Started	
Time Ended	
Date	

Item	Time	Events/Incidents	Actions Taken	Notes

Name _____Signature_____

BUSINESS EVENT

Name of Event	
City,	
State/Zip	
Telephone	
Time Started	
Time Ended	
Date	

Item	Time	Events/Incidents	Actions Taken	Notes

Name _____Signature_____

BUSINESS EVENT

Name of Event	
City,	
State/Zip	
Telephone	
Time Started	
Time Ended	
Date	

Item	Time	Events/Incidents	Actions Taken	Notes

Name _____ Signature _____

BUSINESS EVENT

Name of Event	
City,	
State/Zip	
Telephone	
Time Started	
Time Ended	
Date	

Item	Time	Events/Incidents	Actions Taken	Notes

Name _____Signature_____

BUSINESS EVENT

Name of Event	
City,	
State/Zip	
Telephone	
Time Started	
Time Ended	
Date	

Item	Time	Events/Incidents	Actions Taken	Notes

Name _____Signature_____

BUSINESS EVENT

Name of Event	
City,	
State/Zip	
Telephone	
Time Started	
Time Ended	
Date	

Item	Time	Events/Incidents	Actions Taken	Notes

Name _____ Signature _____

BUSINESS EVENT

Name of Event	
City,	
State/Zip	
Telephone	
Time Started	
Time Ended	
Date	

Item	Time	Events/Incidents	Actions Taken	Notes

Name _____Signature_____

BUSINESS EVENT

Name of Event	
City,	
State/Zip	
Telephone	
Time Started	
Time Ended	
Date	

Item	Time	Events/Incidents	Actions Taken	Notes

Name _____ Signature_____

BUSINESS EVENT

Name of Event	
City,	
State/Zip	
Telephone	
Time Started	
Time Ended	
Date	

Item	Time	Events/Incidents	Actions Taken	Notes

Name _____ Signature_____

BUSINESS EVENT

Name of Event	
City,	
State/Zip	
Telephone	
Time Started	
Time Ended	
Date	

Item	Time	Events/Incidents	Actions Taken	Notes

Name _____ Signature_____

BUSINESS EVENT

Name of Event	
City,	
State/Zip	
Telephone	
Time Started	
Time Ended	
Date	

Item	Time	Events/Incidents	Actions Taken	Notes

Name _____Signature_____

BUSINESS EVENT

Name of Event	
City,	
State/Zip	
Telephone	
Time Started	
Time Ended	
Date	

Item	Time	Events/Incidents	Actions Taken	Notes

Name _____Signature_____

BUSINESS EVENT

Name of Event	
City,	
State/Zip	
Telephone	
Time Started	
Time Ended	
Date	

Item	Time	Events/Incidents	Actions Taken	Notes

Name _____ Signature _____

BUSINESS EVENT

Name of Event	
City,	
State/Zip	
Telephone	
Time Started	
Time Ended	
Date	

Item	Time	Events/Incidents	Actions Taken	Notes

Name _____Signature_____

BUSINESS EVENT

Name of Event	
City,	
State/Zip	
Telephone	
Time Started	
Time Ended	
Date	

Item	Time	Events/Incidents	Actions Taken	Notes

Name _____ Signature _____

BUSINESS EVENT

Name of Event	
City,	
State/Zip	
Telephone	
Time Started	
Time Ended	
Date	

Item	Time	Events/Incidents	Actions Taken	Notes

Name _____ Signature_____

BUSINESS EVENT

Name of Event	
City,	
State/Zip	
Telephone	
Time Started	
Time Ended	
Date	

Item	Time	Events/Incidents	Actions Taken	Notes

Name _____Signature_____

BUSINESS EVENT

Name of Event	
City,	
State/Zip	
Telephone	
Time Started	
Time Ended	
Date	

Item	Time	Events/Incidents	Actions Taken	Notes

Name _____Signature_____

BUSINESS EVENT

Name of Event	
City,	
State/Zip	
Telephone	
Time Started	
Time Ended	
Date	

Item	Time	Events/Incidents	Actions Taken	Notes

Name _____Signature_____

BUSINESS EVENT

Name of Event	
City,	
State/Zip	
Telephone	
Time Started	
Time Ended	
Date	

Item	Time	Events/Incidents	Actions Taken	Notes

Name _____Signature_____

BUSINESS EVENT

Name of Event	
City,	
State/Zip	
Telephone	
Time Started	
Time Ended	
Date	

Item	Time	Events/Incidents	Actions Taken	Notes

Name _____ Signature_____

BUSINESS EVENT

Name of Event	
City,	
State/Zip	
Telephone	
Time Started	
Time Ended	
Date	

Item	Time	Events/Incidents	Actions Taken	Notes

Name _____ Signature_____

BUSINESS EVENT

Name of Event	
City,	
State/Zip	
Telephone	
Time Started	
Time Ended	
Date	

Item	Time	Events/Incidents	Actions Taken	Notes

Name _____Signature_____

BUSINESS EVENT

Name of Event	
City,	
State/Zip	
Telephone	
Time Started	
Time Ended	
Date	

Item	Time	Events/Incidents	Actions Taken	Notes

Name _____Signature_____

BUSINESS EVENT

Name of Event	
City,	
State/Zip	
Telephone	
Time Started	
Time Ended	
Date	

Item	Time	Events/Incidents	Actions Taken	Notes

Name _____ Signature _____

BUSINESS EVENT

Name of Event	
City,	
State/Zip	
Telephone	
Time Started	
Time Ended	
Date	

Item	Time	Events/Incidents	Actions Taken	Notes

Name _____Signature_____

BUSINESS EVENT

Name of Event	
City,	
State/Zip	
Telephone	
Time Started	
Time Ended	
Date	

Item	Time	Events/Incidents	Actions Taken	Notes

Name _____Signature_____

BUSINESS EVENT

Name of Event	
City,	
State/Zip	
Telephone	
Time Started	
Time Ended	
Date	

Item	Time	Events/Incidents	Actions Taken	Notes

Name _____ Signature_____

BUSINESS EVENT

Name of Event	
City,	
State/Zip	
Telephone	
Time Started	
Time Ended	
Date	

Item	Time	Events/Incidents	Actions Taken	Notes

Name _____Signature_____

BUSINESS EVENT

Name of Event	
City,	
State/Zip	
Telephone	
Time Started	
Time Ended	
Date	

Item	Time	Events/Incidents	Actions Taken	Notes

Name _____Signature_____

BUSINESS EVENT

Name of Event	
City,	
State/Zip	
Telephone	
Time Started	
Time Ended	
Date	

Item	Time	Events/Incidents	Actions Taken	Notes

Name _____ Signature _____

BUSINESS EVENT

Name of Event	
City,	
State/Zip	
Telephone	
Time Started	
Time Ended	
Date	

Item	Time	Events/Incidents	Actions Taken	Notes

Name _____Signature_____

BUSINESS EVENT

Name of Event	
City,	
State/Zip	
Telephone	
Time Started	
Time Ended	
Date	

Item	Time	Events/Incidents	Actions Taken	Notes

Name _____ Signature _____

BUSINESS EVENT

Name of Event	
City,	
State/Zip	
Telephone	
Time Started	
Time Ended	
Date	

Item	Time	Events/Incidents	Actions Taken	Notes

Name _____Signature_____

BUSINESS EVENT

Name of Event	
City,	
State/Zip	
Telephone	
Time Started	
Time Ended	
Date	

Item	Time	Events/Incidents	Actions Taken	Notes

Name _____ Signature_____

BUSINESS EVENT

Name of Event	
City,	
State/Zip	
Telephone	
Time Started	
Time Ended	
Date	

Item	Time	Events/Incidents	Actions Taken	Notes

Name _____ Signature_____

BUSINESS EVENT

Name of Event	
City,	
State/Zip	
Telephone	
Time Started	
Time Ended	
Date	

Item	Time	Events/Incidents	Actions Taken	Notes

Name _____ Signature _____

BUSINESS EVENT

Name of Event	
City,	
State/Zip	
Telephone	
Time Started	
Time Ended	
Date	

Item	Time	Events/Incidents	Actions Taken	Notes

Name _____Signature_____

BUSINESS EVENT

Name of Event	
City,	
State/Zip	
Telephone	
Time Started	
Time Ended	
Date	

Item	Time	Events/Incidents	Actions Taken	Notes

Name _____Signature_____

BUSINESS EVENT

Name of Event	
City,	
State/Zip	
Telephone	
Time Started	
Time Ended	
Date	

Item	Time	Events/Incidents	Actions Taken	Notes

Name _____ Signature_____

BUSINESS EVENT

Name of Event	
City,	
State/Zip	
Telephone	
Time Started	
Time Ended	
Date	

Item	Time	Events/Incidents	Actions Taken	Notes

Name _____ Signature _____

BUSINESS EVENT

Name of Event	
City,	
State/Zip	
Telephone	
Time Started	
Time Ended	
Date	

Item	Time	Events/Incidents	Actions Taken	Notes

Name _____Signature_____

BUSINESS EVENT

Name of Event	
City,	
State/Zip	
Telephone	
Time Started	
Time Ended	
Date	

Item	Time	Events/Incidents	Actions Taken	Notes

Name _____Signature_____

BUSINESS EVENT

Name of Event	
City,	
State/Zip	
Telephone	
Time Started	
Time Ended	
Date	

Item	Time	Events/Incidents	Actions Taken	Notes

Name _____Signature_____

BUSINESS EVENT

Name of Event	
City,	
State/Zip	
Telephone	
Time Started	
Time Ended	
Date	

Item	Time	Events/Incidents	Actions Taken	Notes

Name _____ Signature _____

BUSINESS EVENT

Name of Event	
City,	
State/Zip	
Telephone	
Time Started	
Time Ended	
Date	

Item	Time	Events/Incidents	Actions Taken	Notes

Name _____ Signature _____

BUSINESS EVENT

Name of Event	
City,	
State/Zip	
Telephone	
Time Started	
Time Ended	
Date	

Item	Time	Events/Incidents	Actions Taken	Notes

Name _____Signature_____

BUSINESS EVENT

Name of Event	
City,	
State/Zip	
Telephone	
Time Started	
Time Ended	
Date	

Item	Time	Events/Incidents	Actions Taken	Notes

Name _____ Signature_____

BUSINESS EVENT

Name of Event	
City,	
State/Zip	
Telephone	
Time Started	
Time Ended	
Date	

Item	Time	Events/Incidents	Actions Taken	Notes

Name _____Signature_____

BUSINESS EVENT

Name of Event	
City,	
State/Zip	
Telephone	
Time Started	
Time Ended	
Date	

Item	Time	Events/Incidents	Actions Taken	Notes

Name _____ Signature_____

BUSINESS EVENT

Name of Event	
City,	
State/Zip	
Telephone	
Time Started	
Time Ended	
Date	

Item	Time	Events/Incidents	Actions Taken	Notes

Name _____ Signature _____

BUSINESS EVENT

Name of Event	
City,	
State/Zip	
Telephone	
Time Started	
Time Ended	
Date	

Item	Time	Events/Incidents	Actions Taken	Notes

Name _____Signature_____

BUSINESS EVENT

Name of Event	
City,	
State/Zip	
Telephone	
Time Started	
Time Ended	
Date	

Item	Time	Events/Incidents	Actions Taken	Notes

Name _____ Signature _____

BUSINESS EVENT

Name of Event	
City,	
State/Zip	
Telephone	
Time Started	
Time Ended	
Date	

Item	Time	Events/Incidents	Actions Taken	Notes

Name _____Signature_____

BUSINESS EVENT

Name of Event	
City,	
State/Zip	
Telephone	
Time Started	
Time Ended	
Date	

Item	Time	Events/Incidents	Actions Taken	Notes

Name _____Signature_____

BUSINESS EVENT

Name of Event	
City,	
State/Zip	
Telephone	
Time Started	
Time Ended	
Date	

Item	Time	Events/Incidents	Actions Taken	Notes

Name _____ Signature_____

BUSINESS EVENT

Name of Event	
City,	
State/Zip	
Telephone	
Time Started	
Time Ended	
Date	

Item	Time	Events/Incidents	Actions Taken	Notes

Name _____Signature_____

BUSINESS EVENT

Name of Event	
City,	
State/Zip	
Telephone	
Time Started	
Time Ended	
Date	

Item	Time	Events/Incidents	Actions Taken	Notes

Name _____ Signature_____

BUSINESS EVENT

Name of Event	
City,	
State/Zip	
Telephone	
Time Started	
Time Ended	
Date	

Item	Time	Events/Incidents	Actions Taken	Notes

Name _____ Signature_____

BUSINESS EVENT

Name of Event	
City,	
State/Zip	
Telephone	
Time Started	
Time Ended	
Date	

Item	Time	Events/Incidents	Actions Taken	Notes

Name _____ Signature_____

BUSINESS EVENT

Name of Event	
City,	
State/Zip	
Telephone	
Time Started	
Time Ended	
Date	

Item	Time	Events/Incidents	Actions Taken	Notes

Name _____Signature_____

BUSINESS EVENT

Name of Event	
City,	
State/Zip	
Telephone	
Time Started	
Time Ended	
Date	

Item	Time	Events/Incidents	Actions Taken	Notes

Name _____ Signature _____

BUSINESS EVENT

Name of Event	
City,	
State/Zip	
Telephone	
Time Started	
Time Ended	
Date	

Item	Time	Events/Incidents	Actions Taken	Notes

Name _____Signature_____

BUSINESS EVENT

Name of Event	
City,	
State/Zip	
Telephone	
Time Started	
Time Ended	
Date	

Item	Time	Events/Incidents	Actions Taken	Notes

Name _____ Signature_____

BUSINESS EVENT

Name of Event	
City,	
State/Zip	
Telephone	
Time Started	
Time Ended	
Date	

Item	Time	Events/Incidents	Actions Taken	Notes

Name _____Signature_____

BUSINESS EVENT

Name of Event	
City,	
State/Zip	
Telephone	
Time Started	
Time Ended	
Date	

Item	Time	Events/Incidents	Actions Taken	Notes

Name _____ Signature _____

BUSINESS EVENT

Name of Event	
City,	
State/Zip	
Telephone	
Time Started	
Time Ended	
Date	

Item	Time	Events/Incidents	Actions Taken	Notes

Name _____ Signature _____

BUSINESS EVENT

Name of Event	
City,	
State/Zip	
Telephone	
Time Started	
Time Ended	
Date	

Item	Time	Events/Incidents	Actions Taken	Notes

Name _____Signature_____

BUSINESS EVENT

Name of Event	
City,	
State/Zip	
Telephone	
Time Started	
Time Ended	
Date	

Item	Time	Events/Incidents	Actions Taken	Notes

Name _____Signature_____

BUSINESS EVENT

Name of Event	
City,	
State/Zip	
Telephone	
Time Started	
Time Ended	
Date	

Item	Time	Events/Incidents	Actions Taken	Notes

Name _____ Signature _____

BUSINESS EVENT

Name of Event	
City,	
State/Zip	
Telephone	
Time Started	
Time Ended	
Date	

Item	Time	Events/Incidents	Actions Taken	Notes

Name _____Signature_____

BUSINESS EVENT

Name of Event	
City,	
State/Zip	
Telephone	
Time Started	
Time Ended	
Date	

Item	Time	Events/Incidents	Actions Taken	Notes

Name _____Signature_____

BUSINESS EVENT

Name of Event	
City,	
State/Zip	
Telephone	
Time Started	
Time Ended	
Date	

Item	Time	Events/Incidents	Actions Taken	Notes

Name _____Signature_____

BUSINESS EVENT

Name of Event	
City,	
State/Zip	
Telephone	
Time Started	
Time Ended	
Date	

Item	Time	Events/Incidents	Actions Taken	Notes

Name _____Signature_____

BUSINESS EVENT

Name of Event	
City,	
State/Zip	
Telephone	
Time Started	
Time Ended	
Date	

Item	Time	Events/Incidents	Actions Taken	Notes

Name _____ Signature_____

BUSINESS EVENT

Name of Event	
City,	
State/Zip	
Telephone	
Time Started	
Time Ended	
Date	

Item	Time	Events/Incidents	Actions Taken	Notes

Name _____ Signature_____

BUSINESS EVENT

Name of Event	
City,	
State/Zip	
Telephone	
Time Started	
Time Ended	
Date	

Item	Time	Events/Incidents	Actions Taken	Notes

Name _____Signature_____

BUSINESS EVENT

Name of Event	
City,	
State/Zip	
Telephone	
Time Started	
Time Ended	
Date	

Item	Time	Events/Incidents	Actions Taken	Notes

Name _____ Signature _____

BUSINESS EVENT

Name of Event	
City,	
State/Zip	
Telephone	
Time Started	
Time Ended	
Date	

Item	Time	Events/Incidents	Actions Taken	Notes

Name _____Signature_____

BUSINESS EVENT

Name of Event	
City,	
State/Zip	
Telephone	
Time Started	
Time Ended	
Date	

Item	Time	Events/Incidents	Actions Taken	Notes

Name _____ Signature_____

BUSINESS EVENT

Name of Event	
City,	
State/Zip	
Telephone	
Time Started	
Time Ended	
Date	

Item	Time	Events/Incidents	Actions Taken	Notes

Name _____Signature_____

BUSINESS EVENT

Name of Event	
City,	
State/Zip	
Telephone	
Time Started	
Time Ended	
Date	

Item	Time	Events/Incidents	Actions Taken	Notes

Name _____Signature_____

www.ingramcontent.com/pod-product-compliance
Lightning Source LLC
Chambersburg PA
CBHW081114180526
45170CB00008B/2838